Blairs... P9-DBP-311

Blairsville, ...or High School

Blairsville, Pennsylvania

516
R

4342

DATE DUE

MAY 15			
MAR 2 5 1993			
APR 1 6 1997			
GAYLORD			PRINTED IN U.S.A.

Symmetry

EXPLORING MATHEMATICS

by Arthur G. Razzell and K. G. O. Watts

Illustrated by Ellen Raskin

Blairsville Junior High School
Blairsville, Pennsylvania

Doubleday & Company, Inc.
Garden City, New York

4342

516
Raz

Library of Congress Catalog Card Number 67-19124
Illustrations Copyright © 1968 by Ellen Raskin
Text Copyright © 1964 by Arthur G. Razzell and K. G. O. Watts
All Rights Reserved
Printed in the United States of America
First Edition in the United States of America

Tiger! Tiger! burning bright
In the forests of the night,
What immortal hand or eye
Could frame they fearful symmetry?

William Blake (1757–1827)

Blairsville Junior High School
Blairsville, Pennsylvania

Almost everyone has made an ink blot at one time or another. But have you ever folded your paper after making an ink blot and come up with a symmetrical pattern like this? Doing this experiment is an excellent way to begin to understand something about symmetry. But there's a lot more to symmetry than ink blots on paper.

From the beginning of history man has been surrounded by symmetry in the world of nature.

The leaves on most of the trees in the world are symmetrical in shape.

Most fruits, berries, and seeds which man sees or eats are symmetrical.

Butterflies and moths have wings that are balanced in size, shape, and coloring. So have birds and bees and beetles.

Early man may have noticed symmetry in the animals he trapped and hunted, or in those he domesticated and kept. When he learned to cultivate grain he could see symmetry in the beauty of an ear of wheat. And early man must certainly have noticed the physical symmetry of the other people he lived with.

With so many things in the world of nature carefully balanced, it is no wonder that men have been strongly influenced by symmetry in all they have made, designed, and shaped.

Over forty-five hundred years ago Etemena, King of Lagash, a city in what is now the Near East, ordered his silversmith to make a new silver vase. The silversmith decorated the vase with pictures of flying eagles, but instead of drawing an eagle as one might see it in flight he was more concerned in his engraving to show a balance of left side and right side.

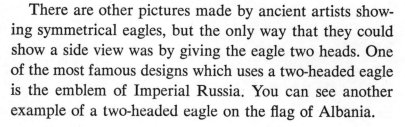

There are other pictures made by ancient artists showing symmetrical eagles, but the only way that they could show a side view was by giving the eagle two heads. One of the most famous designs which uses a two-headed eagle is the emblem of Imperial Russia. You can see another example of a two-headed eagle on the flag of Albania.

The artists and artisans of ancient Egypt used symmetry in their design of carvings and temples. They felt it made their work more beautiful. This entranceway to one of their temples is symmetrical.

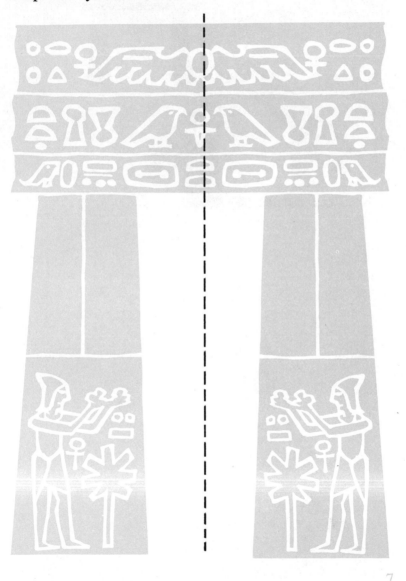

When we look at the buildings made by men at different times in history we can see how very often they used symmetrical designs. We see it in Japan, in New Zealand, in Greece, and in North America. Even modern houses are often symmetrical.

Symmetry may make things look pleasing to the eye, but it often serves a necessary function as well. Imagine that the three columns on the left of the Grecian temple in the illustration were shorter than the three on the right. Not only would the structure look odd, the roof would be in danger of collapse!

Let us look at a symmetrical shape you see very often—the human face. The dotted line drawn on this face is called the axis of symmetry. The eye and ear on one side of the axis are balanced by the eye and ear on the other side. The nose and mouth are balanced neatly in the middle.

However, the human face, like so many other symmetrical objects, has only one **axis of symmetry.** If we turn the head sideways we can see the nose, part of the mouth, and one eye all on one side. The back of the head is on the other side. From this view, the human head is certainly not symmetrical.

For the drawing to be symmetrical, we would need two faces like this.

The idea of the two-faced human head is not new. The Romans had a god named Janus who was the god of doorways and gates. He was always pictured with two faces so that he could supervise both the insides and outsides of houses, or the entrances and exits of public buildings. He was also regarded as the god of arrival and departure. He is celebrated with the arrival of each new year, since the Romans named January in his honor. His symmetrical two-faced head appears on many Roman coins.

Most of the things we have looked at in this book are symmetrical on one axis, for this is the most common form of symmetry we see in the world around us. The name given to this kind of symmetry is **bilateral symmetry.** *Bi* in Latin means two, *lateral* means side, so the name means two-sided symmetry. The axis of bilateral symmetry runs along the water's edge in this picture.

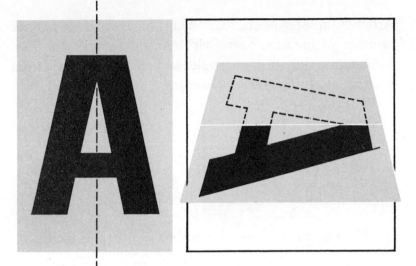

A simple experiment with a small mirror will help you to understand more clearly what bilateral symmetry means. Draw a large letter A on a sheet of paper. Put in the axis of symmetry and cut along it with a pair of scissors. Hold the paper close to the mirror in the way shown in the drawing and you will see that the reflected image will make the letter appear complete.

ABCDEFGHIJKLMNOPQRSTUVWXYZ

Here is a complete alphabet. In the type used, fifteen of the letters are symmetrical. Which ones are they? Some letters of the alphabet can be made in different ways. When you ordinarily print capital letters in your own handwriting, how many of them do you print symmetrically? Print the alphabet on a sheet of paper and mark the axis of symmetry on all of the letters you can. Make the letters very large so you can test your accuracy with a mirror.

Although most symmetrical objects have only one axis of symmetry, there are some with more than one axis. The equilateral triangle (a triangle with three sides of equal length), has three axes of symmetry.

Here is one,   here is another,   here is the third.

Use this picture as a guide to draw an equilateral triangle on a piece of thin, stiff cardboard. Attach some thin string to your triangle so that it lies along one of the axes, as you see in the illustration. Hold the thread taut and get a friend to spin the triangle. What shape does it appear to form in space?

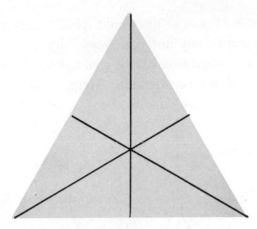

Now draw in all three axes of symmetry. They meet at one point in the equilateral triangle. This point is called the **center of symmetry.** Stick a pin through the center of symmetry of your cardboard triangle and spin the triangle around very quickly. Can you see what shape it appears to form when it is spinning?

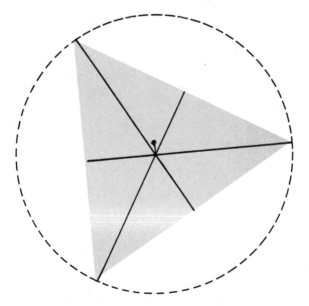

If you make a list of things you discover having three axes of symmetry, it may not be a very long one. A northern part of Italy, called Lombardy, was famous at one time for its bankers and moneylenders. Here is the coat of arms of Lombardy, which can still be seen outside some pawnbrokers' shops.

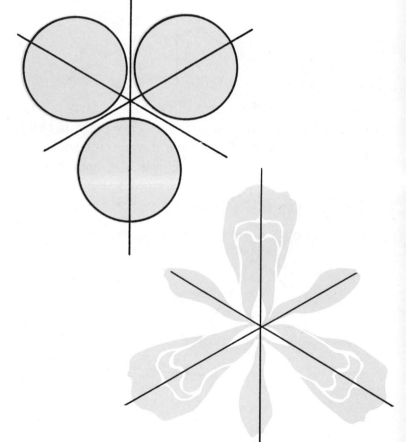

The iris has three axes of symmetry. So have some airplane propellers. Can you discover other things with three axes of symmetry?

The square has four axes of symmetry. Here are two:

The diagonals of the square make the other two axes.

17

Blairsville Junior High School
Blairsville, Pennsylvania

Cut a square from a sheet of cardboard and fix a thread to lie along one of the axes of symmetry as shown in the drawing below. Spin it as you did the triangle. What shape does it appear to form in space? Next fix a thread along the diagonal axis of symmetry. What shape do you see when you spin it now?

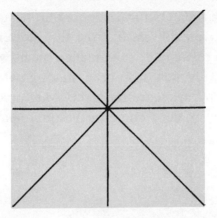

All the axes pass through the Center of Symmetry. Put a pin through the Center of Symmetry in your square. Spin it as you did the triangle. What shape does it appear to form?

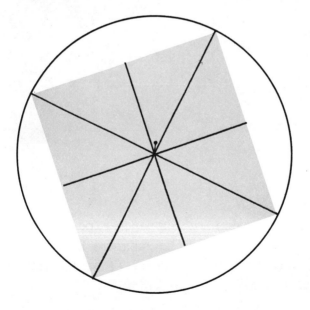

There are not many natural objects that have four axes of symmetry. A few flowers like the tiny flower of the dogwood do. There are more man-made objects with four axes of symmetry, for men have been making patterns and designs based on the square for a very long time. You might try designing some symmetrical square-patterned tiles yourself.

You can also use scissors to cut symmetrical patterns out of paper squares.

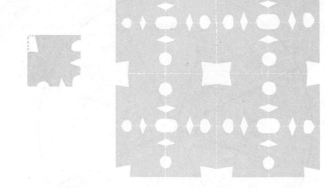

Using a 6-inch square of thin paper, experiment with symmetrical paper folding. The Japanese have made paper folding into an art, called origami. These illustrations show you how to make an origami bird.

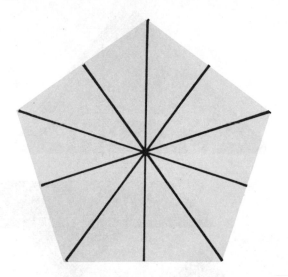

The five-sided regular *pentagon* has five axes of symmetry. There are a great many beautiful flowers that also have five axes. Most of us have seen a five-pointed starfish on the beach. The pattern on the shell of a sea urchin is also repeated in five identical sections. The building on the outskirts of Washington, D.C., which houses the Department of Defense is called the Pentagon because it has five sides.

The *pentagram,* which is a star pentagon, has been known for thousands of years. It was the badge of the Pythagorean Brotherhood, which was a group of learned Greek mathematicians who worked and studied with Pythagoras. Although it looks more complicated, it is composed of the same number of straight lines as the pentagon. It too has five axes of symmetry. Note that the pentagram has a pentagon within it and that it is possible to keep on repeating the pattern of symbol within symbol.

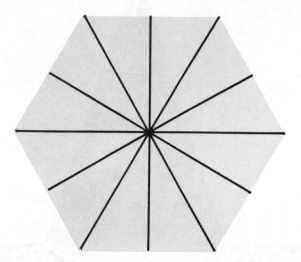

This is a regular *hexagon*. It has six sides and six axes of symmetry. You may recognize it as the shape of the top of bee and wasp cells.

There is no end to the number of patterns that can be made within the hexagon. Next time there is a snowfall try to catch some snowflakes on a piece of cold, dark cloth. You can see the pattern of their hexagonal structure with the naked eye, but they look much finer under a magnifying glass.

There is only one shape you can draw on paper that has an infinite number of axes of symmetry and that is the circle. No matter how many axes you draw, there are always more that can be drawn. When you have drawn these, there are always others that might be drawn between them.

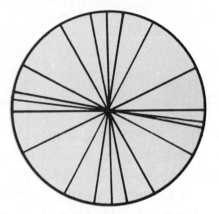

Cut a circle out of cardboard and fix a thread to lie along one of the axes of symmetry. Then spin the circle on the thread. What shape does it appear to form?

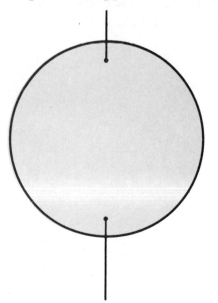

Make a set of cut-out cardboard shapes of the regular figures we have been looking at. You already have an equilateral triangle and a square. A pentagon is quite difficult to draw. One way to make a small pentagon is by tying a simple knot in a very long, thin strip of paper as you see in the diagram. You can make a hexagon by using your equilateral triangle twice—once right side up and once upside down. As you see in the illustration, by connecting the six points you will have a hexagon.

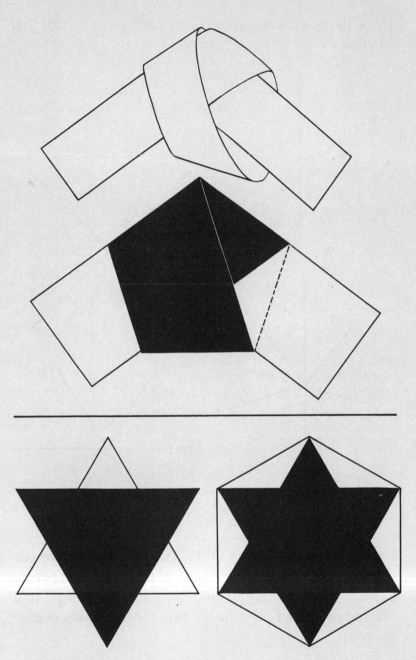

Draw in the axes of symmetry on each shape so that you can find the center of symmetry.

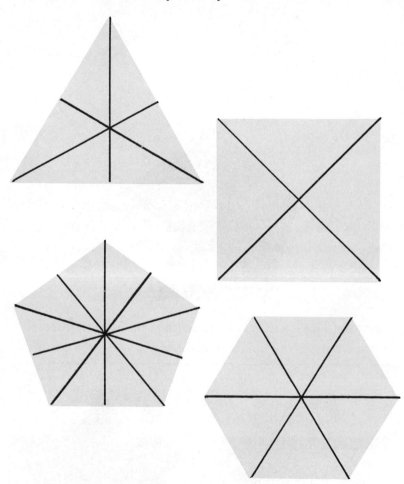

Earlier in the book we spun the triangle around its center of symmetry very quickly to look at the shape it appeared to make when it was spinning. Now pin the triangle to a sheet of paper and examine the movement it makes in slow motion.

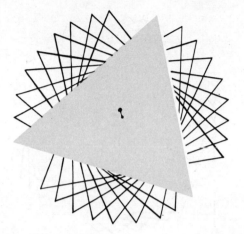

Trace around the triangle with a pencil. Rotate it a little and trace around it again. Keep on doing this in the way shown in the drawing. You will find that you have made a circular crisscross pattern when the triangle has been rotated only a third of the way around.

Try it with a square next. The pattern will be complete after it has been rotated only a quarter of the way around.

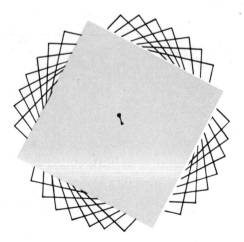

29

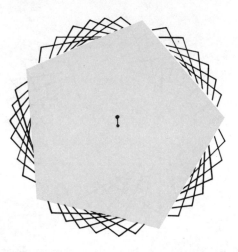

If you trace around the pentagon in a similar way the circular pattern will be complete after it has been rotated only a fifth of the way around; the hexagon will only need to be rotated a sixth of the way.

Why was it that the circular patterns were completed without rotating the shapes around a full circle?

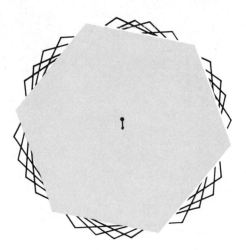

The regular shapes we have been working with have more than one kind of symmetry.

The equilateral triangle has bilateral symmetry—you can see that the left side of the triangle can be folded over to fit exactly over the right side. When the triangle is rotated you can also see that it appears identical in three different positions. This is called **rotational symmetry.**

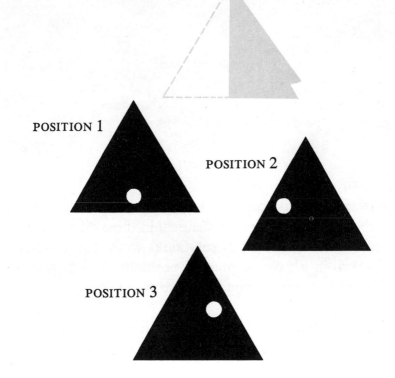

POSITION 1

POSITION 2

POSITION 3

Here the triangle has been drawn with a different side as a base each time. If there weren't a dot next to one of the sides you wouldn't be able to tell which position was which.

POSITION 1

POSITION 2

POSITION 3

This triangle has been drawn with an angle at the bottom each time. It also appears identical in three different positions. When a figure has rotational symmetry it appears identical in a fixed number of positions. This is true no matter what position you choose to start with.

When you made the circular pattern using the triangle you rotated the triangle from Position 1 to Position 2 in one third of a turn, and Position 2 appears identical to your starting position. A square appears identical in four different positions. In how many positions does a pentagon appear identical? What about a hexagon?

These four pictures show you how Rotational Symmetry differs from Bilateral Symmetry.

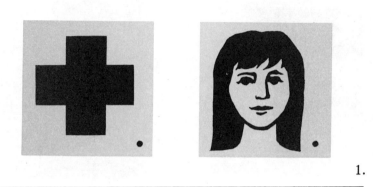

1.

Picture 1 shows a square with a girl's head in it. This head has Bilateral Symmetry. Next to it is a square with a cross in it. This has Rotational Symmetry, in addition to Bilateral Symmetry. In picture 2 both squares have been rotated a quarter of the way around. The girl's head now appears sideways, but the cross looks just the same. In picture 3 the squares have been turned once more. Now the girl's head is upside down but the cross still looks just the same. Picture 4 shows the squares when they have been rotated again. The girl's head appears in a different position, but the cross *still* looks the same.

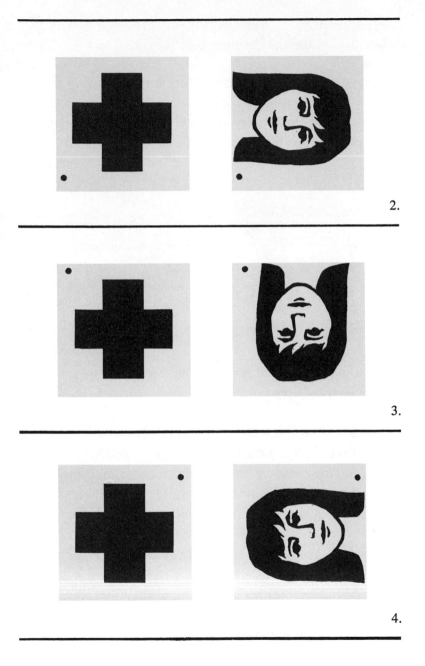

2.

3.

4.

ABCDEFGHIJKLMNOPQRSTUVWXYZ

At this point, it might be interesting for you to reexamine symmetry in the letters of the alphabet. Now that you know about rotational symmetry you will find three more letters in this alphabet to be symmetrical.

Some of the letters that have bilateral symmetry also have rotational symmetry.

Most of the things that have rotational symmetry *also* have bilateral symmetry. This is true of your cardboard cut-out shapes and the cross we have just been experimenting with. Only a very few objects have rotational symmetry without bilateral symmetry. Let us look at one example.

This triangular shape is called a running symbol—which is the symbol for the Isle of Man. Like the cross it can be revolved around a central point and it gives three identical positions of rotational symmetry, but unlike the cross it has no axis of bilateral symmetry.

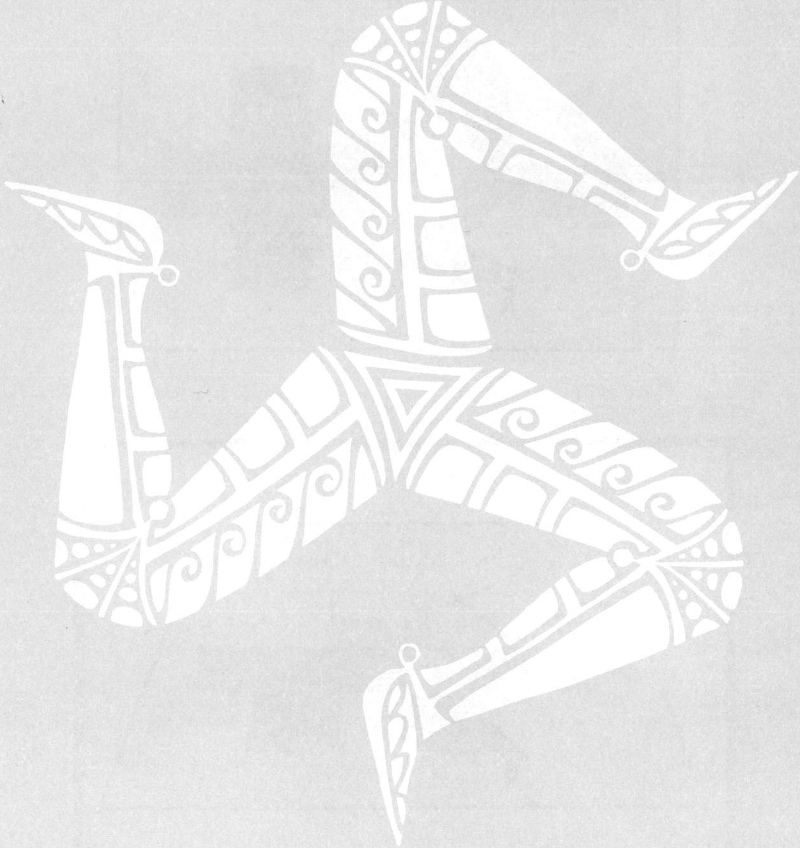

Draw a cross and a running symbol on a piece of paper and cut them both in half. Hold one half of the paper in front of the mirror. The cross is complete in its reflected image because it has bilateral symmetry.

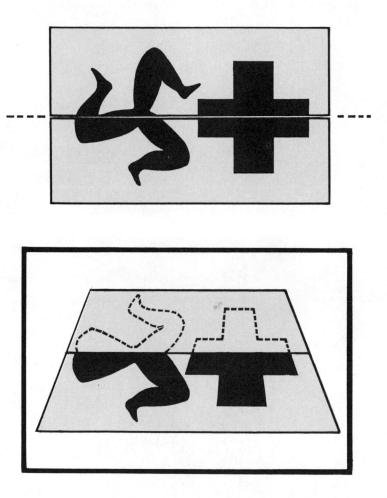

The running symbol fails this mirror test for bilateral symmetry completely. It has only rotational symmetry.

The swastika, an ancient symbol with a much longer history than the German Nazis, is another figure which has Rotational Symmetry but no axis of Bilateral Symmetry. Perhaps it is this strange, incomplete symmetry that has made the swastika a symbol man has used for many, many centuries. Some wheels are made with a shape in the center that has Rotational Symmetry but not Bilateral Symmetry. You might see one on the wheel of an old sewing machine.

Solid figures can have rotational axes of symmetry too. A pine cone is an excellent and beautiful example.

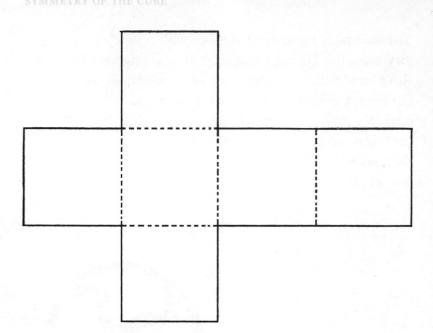

The cube has several different axes of symmetry and you can best study them by making a cardboard cube for yourself. Here is the pattern you need to draw on thin cardboard. Cut it out and fold it along the dotted lines. You can use cellophane tape or masking tape to stick along the edges of the cube to hold it together. In order to keep track of which side is which, it is a good idea to color each face of the cube differently.

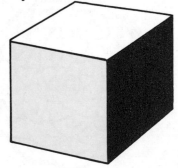

To show that a cube has Rotational Symmetry, carefully push a knitting needle through the center of one of the faces and out through the center of the opposite face. Be careful of your fingers as you do this.

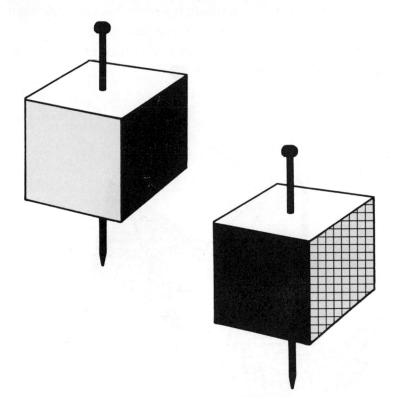

Begin with any side, or corner facing you and rotate the cube around the needle. In one quarter of a turn it will have reached a position that looks just the same as the position you started from. On this axis there are four different positions in which the cube will appear the same. The cube has three axes similar to the one you have seen. Can you find the other two?

Now take your knitting needle and push it down through one corner of the cube and out through the opposite corner. This is a different axis of symmetry. Not only does the cube look different in this position, but it also acts differently when you rotate it. If you rotate it slowly one complete turn on this axis, you will find there are just three positions in which it looks the same. The cube has four axes like this. Can you find the other three?

The cube has still one more kind of rotational axis of symmetry to be looked at. Push your knitting needle through the middle of one edge and out through the opposite edge. There are only two positions on this axis where the cube has an identical appearance; however, there are six of these axes. Can you find them?

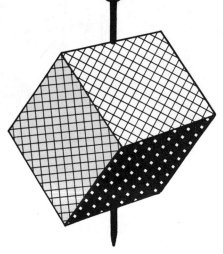

43

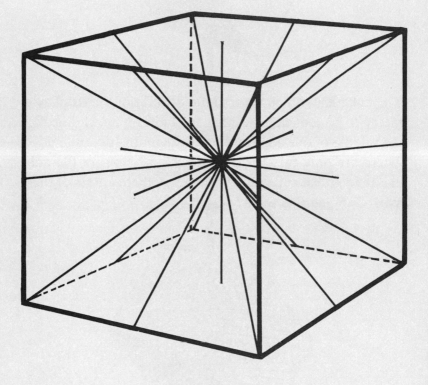

Here is a drawing of a cube showing all the possible axes of symmetry.

You might try to make some other solid figures and find their axes of symmetry. Here is a pattern for a pyramid made of equilateral triangles. How many axes of symmetry can you find in it?

You already know that there are an infinite number of axes of symmetry in a circle. It should be no surprise then for you to see that there are also an infinite number of axes of symmetry in a sphere.

Many common objects look most unusual if we see just a section of them and their axes of symmetry. This is a section of a flower pot and its axis is shown as a dotted line. If we could rotate this section very quickly around the axis it would take up its more usual appearance.

Look carefully at these puzzle pictures and see if you can draw the complete object. In each case the axis of symmetry is shown as a dotted line.

Perhaps you can arrange an exhibition of symmetry in your classroom. You could display a collection of symmetrical objects and behind it pictures and patterns you have made. You'll probably be surprised at how many good illustrations of symmetry that you can find in newspapers and magazines by keeping your eyes open and looking at things closely and thoroughly.

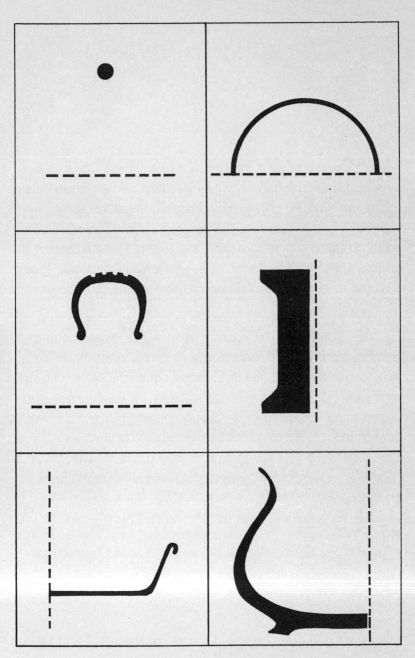

ARTHUR RAZZELL and K.G.O. WATTS are two Englishmen, presently living in London and teaching education in schools there. Mr. Razzell, born in Kent, was married after serving in the Second World War and has three children—two boys and a girl. Mr. Watts served as a radar mechanic in the Royal Air Force. Originally from Hampshire, he is married and has two young children.

ELLEN RASKIN was born in Milwaukee, Wisconsin, and lived there until she went to the University of Wisconsin. While still in college she decided on art as a career, and she has been extraordinarily successful. Miss Raskin has illustrated many children's books—a recent project is a beautiful edition of William Blake's *Songs of Innocence* which she illustrated and set to music. She has also done over a thousand book jackets, plus magazine and advertising illustrations.

Miss Raskin now lives in New York City.

Blair .... nigh School

Blairsville, Pennsylvania